Understanding Business Statistics

Gareth Lewis

BARRON'S

All inquiries should be addressed to:
Barron's Educational Series, Inc.
250 Wireless Boulevard
Hauppauge, New York 11788

Library of Congress Catalog Card Number 96-6541

International Standard Book No. 0-7641-0257-5

Library of Congress Cataloging-in-Publication Data
Lewis, Gareth.
Understanding business statistics / Gareth Lewis,
p. cm. — (Barron's business success series)
Includes index.
ISBN 0-7641-0257-5
1. Commercial statistics. I. Title. II. Title: Understanding statistics in a week
HF1017.L426 1997
519.5—dc21 96-6541
CIP

PRINTED IN HONG KONG
9 8 7 6 5 4 3 2 1

Contents

Introduction

We live in an information age, and the world of work requires that we process, organize, present, and interpret large amounts of information. Much of this information is quantitative in nature, and the skills needed are those of statistics.

For many of us, our lack of confidence in tackling mathematics prevents us from acquiring and using the basic ideas and skills necessary to make us fluent with simple business statistics. This is a pity because the skills needed are basic and easily grasped. High-level skill in math is not required.

This book explains those basic ideas and skills to help you build confidence to tackle the many information problems and challenges that arise every day in the business world. It sets out the basic techniques and concepts used for business applications and needs, and it covers them in an easy-to-understand and practical format.

The topics we will look at are

- Statistically Speaking
- Numbers—The Raw Material
- Organizing and Analyzing Information
- Illustrating Data
- Just in Time
- Methods and Techniques
- Applications of Business Statistics

Chapter 1

Statistically Speaking

In this chapter, we will explore the notion of business statistics and what it means to us in our everyday working lives. We will look at the following.

- What is business statistics?
- The processes of business statistics
- Sources of information

WHAT IS BUSINESS STATISTICS?

In the normal course of our working lives we are bombarded by facts and figures, such as these:

1. Customer X has ordered 200 units of product Y.

2. Product Y accounts for 20% of all sales.

Such facts and figures we call *data*, like statement **1** above. Much of the data is numerical, and arises quite naturally out of the work that we do. These facts and figures are often not of great significance, even when we collect hundreds and thousands of them. They become much more interesting and useful to us when we organize, process, and interpret them. When we collect data and use it to make some sense of what is going on in our world, we transform it. It becomes information, and a useful, numerical bit of information—like statement **2** above—we call a *statistic*.

Statistics itself is the branch of mathematics that deals with the processing of data about the world. It is a collection of techniques and processes for manipulating quantitative data.

Business statistics is much more than the uncritical collection of huge amounts of data. This is easy to do, and many organizations collect much more data than they can reasonably or profitably use. Ask yourself how much time you spend looking over large amounts of information that you never actually use. How much space does this useless information take up?

So who *does* put all this information to use, and for what purpose? Almost everyone uses information and the statistics derived from it, and it is applied in almost every aspect of business and working life. Examples include:

- production/operations
- logistics
- customer service

- marketing
- purchasing and supply
- human resource management
- finance

For most people who are not professional statisticians, what is most important is to be able to read and interpret statistics. This requires knowledge and experience of the particular context, together with basic statistical numeracy. The fact that business statistics involves numbers and requires math is enough to bring fear to many people. This is a pity, for at least two reasons.

First, the math involved in the most used and some of the most useful statistics is really quite simple and basic. It is the sort of calculation that even the most mathophobic people learned to master at school. Even if you are still lacking in confidence with the math, you have electronic calculators and computers to do the work for us. The only requirement, then, is to understand what the processes are and how to use them intelligently. (Those simple skills that are required are set out in the next chapter.)

Second, the purpose of this book is not to turn you into an expert statistician. It is not important that you understand and can do all that a professional statistician can do. What is important is that you can do those simple but necessary things that account for 95 percent of your needs, and that you have some appreciation of what the other 5 percent is about.

You may not aspire to the knowledge and skills of the professional expert, but you can read what they tell you with some discrimination, understand the terms that are used, and interpret the information presented.

THE PROCESSES OF BUSINESS STATISTICS

In business statistics, you not only collect the data, you do something with it. You process it to provide information, to solve problems, and to make decisions. These processes, which are basically mathematical, are what business statistics is all about.

The basic processes are as shown in the diagram:

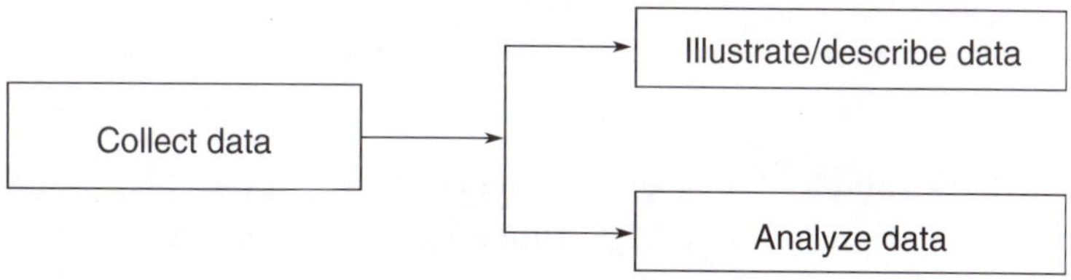

Collect data

Data comes from the normal operational activities of organizations, but also from other sources. They process the data into information, and make it available, either commercially, or free through the public domain. Some of the sources of such information are discussed in the following section.

When acquiring data it is often the case that you can't get it from the whole of a target population. Whether this is about components in a production run, or people, it is often expensive or impractical to collect data on them all. Therefore, a very important principle in statistics is that of sampling. The idea behind sampling is that you pick a small group of people (or components, or whatever) that will have the same characteristics as the total (or parent) population. Most people know of this idea from political polls. If you ask 1,000 people how they will vote at the next election, you want to be able to project that the proportions will be the same for the *total* voting population.

Great care is taken to try to ensure that the sample reflects the characteristics of the parent population. Sampling methods include the following.

- **Random sample.** This is a sample where every member of the population has an equal chance of being selected; there are various ways to achieve this.
- **Stratified sample.** This is where appropriate proportions are randomly selected from a population to reflect its makeup against certain criteria; with people, you might stratify by age, social class, and so on.
- **Quota sample.** Using questionnaires with people, each interviewer is given a quota, and they have to satisfy the quota in their own way, subject to certain criteria.

Some very sophisticated statistics can be applied to measure the confidence with which the sample can be compared to the total population. These will be discussed in Chapter 7.

Illustrate/describe data

Once you have collected the data, you can begin to organize it. This enables you to get a picture of the totality of the information, and to be able to describe its basic features. This ability is enhanced if you use the graphic methods from illustrative statistics. Picturing information in this way helps you to interpret and understand it.

Analyze data

Having collected and organized the data, you can also apply the mathematical techniques that give you the statistics. The latter are the numbers that describe certain aspects or attributes of the collection of data.

These various processes are covered in more detail in the chapters that follow.

SOURCES OF INFORMATION

Before we get to the skills and processes involved, however, we should try to examine where the information we use as raw material comes from. This is important because of the sheer variety and richness of sources, but also because many people are not aware of the huge potential sources of useful information that are available.

The information used for analyses that inform the decisions we make comes in many varieties and from many sources. There are three basic types of information source for use in a business context.

Sources of information

- databases and published sources
- operational information
- research-based information

We will look at each of these in turn.

Databases and published sources

There is a great deal of information out there that has already been collected, organized, and processed. Of course, the sources of this information depend to a great extent on its type and nature. Some examples include:

Government. The U.S. Department of Commerce publishes, through the U.S. Government Printing Office, statistics on population, employment, demographics, and other statistics, based on information from the Census Bureau. Other U.S. government departments also publish statistics based on the responsibilities of each department. For example, the U.S. Department of Justice publishes crime statistics.

The European Community. This provides a huge amount of information (as you might expect). Publications include *European Economy* (on economic statistics, including a *Series A* supplement on economic trends, and *Series B* with business and consumer survey results), *OECD Observer* (a bimonthly magazine with 60 pages of statistics on member countries), and *Economic Outlook* (with analysis, projections, costs, prices, and trade and employment figures).

There are also **commercial sources** of information. These usually offer specialized information at commercial rates. Organizations like Gallup conduct surveys on consumer trends.

Information about companies can be obtained from a number of sources.

Operational information

This is information that is derived from the day-to-day running of organizations. It may take the form of information about output (volume, quality, and so on), sales, or any other aspect of an organization's operations.

Such information, particularly if it relates to customers and markets, can often be among the most valuable assets a company can have. Imagine the value to an insurance company, for instance, of the information it has about its customers' circumstances, habits, and buying preferences, and you will understand that such a marketing database is a very powerful tool.

Research-based information

This is information acquired by an organization to satisfy some particular purpose. It could include market and marketing information, for instance about customers' (or potential customers') habits or needs, or it could provide information about levels of customer satisfaction. Some of this information can be found in published sources (as mentioned on page 8) or gathered by desk or telephone research.

One major way of acquiring information is by the use of *questionnaires*. These involve a structured set of questions designed to elicit useful information. The whole business of questionnaire design is beyond the scope of this book, but there are some useful common-sense notions that should be taken into account when compiling one. These include:

1. Keep questions short. The shorter, the better, as people are more likely to respond and complete. It also helps to keep the information (and analysis) down to manageable proportions.

2. Keep questions unambiguous. To check that you will not confuse potential respondents, test out the questions first (even if only on colleagues).

3. Keep questions simple. It is surprising how often this is ignored. Questions requiring yes/no answers are obviously the easiest, but they also give limited information. However, questions inviting long, wordy responses rarely lend themselves easily to analysis. There are methods you can use to simplify responses. These include offering choices (a, b, c, d...) or numerical rating scales (*never* to *always*, or *poor* to *excellent*).

SUMMARY

In Chapter 1 we have discussed the nature of business statistics—what it is about and who might use it. We have also defined the basic processes that it involves. They are

- collecting data.
- illustrating and describing data.
- analyzing data.

In addition, we have discussed some ideas about collecting data and have highlighted sources of useful information.

In order for us to begin exploring the basic tools and techniques of business statistics, we now need to set out the basic mathematical and arithmetical skills that are required.

Chapter 2

Numbers—The Raw Material

We now need to turn our attention to the stuff that constitutes virtually all of statistics. This is the point at which some adults turn off—but don't!

Many people whose experience of geometry and algebra at school has helped to convince them that they are no good with math are actually very adept at using and interpreting numbers. Many strongly nonmathematical people can balance their domestic budgets to the penny. Many so-called mathematical failures can work out in three seconds flat that 17, double 12 is a finish from 41 in darts.

Although in this book we will keep the math to a minimum, we *will* ask you to use the everyday facility that you have gained with numbers over many years' experience. The basic and simple operations you have acquired are just about all you need to be statistically numerate and confident.

In this chapter we will look at

- numbers.
- basic operations.
- important measures.

NUMBERS

We all know what numbers are—we use them every day of our lives. The first set of numbers we become familiar with are the simple counting numbers:

1 2 3 4 5 6 7 8 9...

However, for many real applications, these won't suffice on their own. You first need to add the negative numbers to get the set of *integers*:

...–5 –4 –3 –2 –1 0 1 2 3 4 5...

Again, even this set is not sufficient, for now you need to add numbers *in between* the whole numbers. This gives you the set of so-called *real numbers*, which includes the fractions and decimals. Although even this set is not enough for mathematicians, it is enough for almost any purpose you are likely to come across in statistics.

When you start to apply numbers to measuring quantities in the real world, you see that they can apply in different ways. For instance, if you look at any application where you are counting people, you will always be dealing with whole units! Variables like this, that can only take specific values (usually, but not always, whole numbers) are called *discrete*. They jump from one value to another, and there is nothing in between. Shoe size is a good example of this.

There are, however, other kinds of variables where this is not the case. Quantities like temperature, distance, size, pressure, and many more natural quantities can take *any* value. Such variables are called *continuous variables*. Importantly, any measure of a continuous variable is always approximate and depends on the *accuracy* with which you can measure it. With temperature, for instance, the reason you are measuring it, and the instruments you are using, will determine the accuracy you need to measure to. On a steaming hot day, it is enough to know that the temperature is in the 100s to understand why you feel uncomfortable. For a patient in a hospital, you measure temperature to the nearest tenth of a degree. In a scientific experiment, temperatures can be measured and controlled to hundredths and even thousandths of a degree.

Many numbers and real-world measurements are made simpler and more manageable, however, by using estimation and approximation. The most usual way of approximating numbers is by rounding. For instance, with quantities such as money, you might round figures to the nearest $1, and this is fairly easy to do. The only problem is what to do with amounts like $2.50. The convention is that you round such amounts up to the nearest $1. For other purposes you might round to the nearest tenth (the nearest unit decimal place), or the nearest 10, 100, 1,000, or, in some cases, the one million units.

There is another convention with large numbers that helps you simplify them and so work more easily with them. Look at this set of numbers:

	($000's)
$257,000	257
$642,000	642
$312,000	312
$896,000	896

The figures in the right-hand list are much simpler to read and work with than the original figures in the left-hand list.

Another way of using numbers applies to data that is not itself numerical in form. In some cases it helps to artificially make it numerical so that you can then use mathematical techniques to organize, analyze, and illustrate it. Options here include

- rank ordering.
- weighting.
- coding.
- rating scales.

BASIC OPERATIONS

Professional statisticians can and do use a large array of very complex and sophisticated mathematical concepts and techniques—enough to boggle your mind. Research statisticians who test new drugs are a good example.

However, for most of us, the math we need in order to be able to work with, and more importantly interpret, statistics is really quite simple, and was learned in school.

The basic requirements are

- the four rules of number.
- percentages.
- proportions and rates.

The four rules of number

Most of the processing of numerical information that is done in the name of business statistics comes down to the use of the four rules of number. These are the basic operations of addition, subtraction, multiplication, and division. Some people can do substantial amounts of such processing in their heads. Those who can't, have the help of electronic calculators and computers. It should rarely be necessary to laboriously perform large numbers of mechanical operations on paper.

Percentages

One of the most useful and widely used mathematical concepts is that of *percentages*. Almost any statistical context or report mentions percentages, and they appear on almost every page of the newspapers and journals we read every day.

A percentage is a way of expressing a proportion. Per cent literally means per hundred, or in every hundred. In this sense you can think of a percentage as a fraction with a denominator of a hundred. Thus:

$$10\% = \frac{10}{100} \text{ and } 25\% = \frac{25}{100}$$

and so on.

If you turn a percentage into a fraction by dividing by 100, it seems logical to turn a fraction (or a proportion) into a percentage by multiplying by 100. Thus:

$$\frac{2}{5} = \frac{2}{5} \times 100\% = \frac{200}{5} = 40\%$$

If 36 out of 400 people prefer margarine to butter, you can calculate the percentage by first turning it into a fraction:

$$\frac{36}{400} = \frac{36}{400} \times 100\% = 9\%$$

If you calculate 36 ÷ 400 on a calculator you will see that the answer is 0.09. To make this into a percentage, multiply by 100. Nine percent of people thus prefer margarine.

The other figure you often need to calculate is that of a percentage of a given amount. For example, if you want to calculate 15% of $300, this is equivalent to calculating

$$\frac{15}{100} \times \$300 = \frac{(15 \times 300)}{100}$$

So, 8% of $7 is

$$\frac{(8 \times 7)}{100} = 0.56$$

The answer is $0.56 or 56¢.

With inflation ever-present in our economy, we often need to calculate percentage increases—for prices, costs, and so on. We occasionally also need to calculate percentage decreases, for instance for discount rates.

What is the discount price for an $80 item at a 12 percent discount? In other words, what is $80 decreased by 12 percent?

To calculate this you do the following:

- **Step 1** Calculate 12% of $80:
  (12 × 80)/100 = $9.60

- **Step 2** Subtract from $80:
  $80.00 – $9.60 = $70.40

To increase prices (or any other quantity) you follow the same procedure, but add instead of subtract.

It should be noticed that 12 percent of $80 is not the same as $70.40 plus 12 percent. This mistake is often made, and you might like to convince yourself by doing the arithmetic.

Proportions and rates

We have already come across an important proportion: the percentage. But *proportions* don't have to be expressed per hundred; they can be expressed by any fraction. For example, if you want to make 2,000 tons of a substance with chemicals A and B mixed in proportion 2:3, this is how to calculate it. The proportion 2:3 gives you five shares (2 + 3), so you want:

$$\frac{2}{5} \text{ of A and } \frac{3}{5} \text{ of B}$$

$$\frac{2}{5} \times 2{,}000 = (2 \times 2{,}000)/5 = 800 \text{ tons}$$

$$\frac{3}{5} \times 2{,}000 = (3 \times 2{,}000)/5 = 1{,}200 \text{ tons}$$

Rates are the measure of change of one quantity relative to another. They involve real units and quantities measured against each other. Inflation is a rate. It is the rate at which prices are increasing, and it is expressed as a percentage. Inflation can be quite a difficult concept to understand because it is quite abstract. For example, if the rate of inflation is static, perhaps at 4 percent, prices are still, however, moving up.

IMPORTANT MEASURES

Having dealt with the basic operations and concepts that we need with numbers, we can now move on to some important statistical measures. The two we are most interested in are

- measures of central tendency or averages.
- measures of dispersion.

Averages

Averages measure the central tendency of a set of numbers. The use of averages is an attempt to reduce a set of numbers to a central or middle number that is somehow representative of the whole set. For any set of numbers there are three such measures.

The *mean* is what we would normally call the average in everyday language, and it is the most commonly used of the three measures. We obtain it by adding up all of the values and sharing them equally between the number of values. It is very like the center of gravity of a set of numbers.

To calculate the mean of the set of numbers 5 6 8 10 11:

- **Step 1** Add up all of the values:
  5 + 6 + 8 + 10 + 11 = 40

- **Step 2** Divide by the number of values:
  the mean is 40/5 = 8

It is useful to be able to read the mathematical symbols, and an added benefit is that this is a shorthand way of remembering the method.

We use the letter x to denote variables, and the Greek letter Σ (sigma) to mean "sum of." So Σx is the sum of all the values.

We use the letter n to denote the number of values, and the mean itself is denoted by $\overline{x}$.

Using these symbols, we write the mean as

$$\overline{x} = \frac{\Sigma x}{n}$$

The *median* is the number in the middle of the set, when they are arranged in order. In our set 5 6 8 10 11, the value in the middle is 8. In the set 3 4 6 7 9 10, the middle comes between 6 and 7, so it is 6.5.

The *mode* is the most frequently found or most popular value in a set. It can be useful if there are a large number of values. If you were looking at shoe sizes in a class full of children, the modal shoe size might be a more useful average than the mean, both because it is an *actual* shoe size and because it tells us something useful—that more children actually take that size.

With a distribution of incomes, the mode might again tell us more than the mean, because with the mean as a measure the value of a few very large incomes balances out a much larger number of smaller incomes.

Of course, there are limitations in using a single number to describe a set of values. Each one has its uses, and conversely, each one can be *misused* in certain circumstances.

Measures of dispersion

Look at these two sets of numbers:

5 6 8 10 11   1 4 8 12 15

The mean of both sets of numbers is 8, yet the second set of numbers is more spread out. You need a way of describing how spread out a set of values is. This "spread-outness" is called *dispersion.* There are various ways of quantifying this notion of dispersion. The simplest way is called the range. This is quite simply the difference between the largest and the smallest values. Thus, the range for the first set is 11 – 5 = 6. The range for the second set is 15 – 1 = 14.

However, the most important measure of dispersion is called the *standard deviation.* To obtain this you take the average of the distances of the values from the mean. When doing this calculation, you square the distances, so that those negative distances (lower than the mean) don't cancel out the positive distances (higher than the mean).

Here is how to calculate the standard deviation for the first set. We show the calculations in a table.

- **Step 1** Write the values in a column. Add up the values.
- **Step 2** Calculate the mean.
- **Step 3** Calculate the deviations from the mean $(x - \overline{x})$.
- **Step 4** Square the deviations $(x - \overline{x})^2$.
- **Step 5** Take the mean of the squared deviations.
- **Step 6** Take the square root.

Perform Step 5 by adding the squares of the deviations and dividing by n:

$$26/5 = 5.2$$

And for Step 6, the calculation is as follows:

$$\sqrt{5.2} = 2.28$$

x	$(x - \overline{x})$	$(x - \overline{x})^2$
5	–3	9
6	–2	4
8	0	0
10	2	4
11	3	9
$\Sigma x = 40$		$\Sigma(x - \overline{x})^2 = 26$

Now you denote the standard deviation by s; and so, in symbols, it is:

$$s = \sqrt{\frac{\Sigma\,(x - \overline{x})^2}{n}}$$

For the mathematically minded, it is equivalent but simpler to use the formula

$$s = \sqrt{\frac{\Sigma x^2}{n} - \left(\frac{\Sigma x}{n}\right)^2}$$

Armed with these few mathematical operations and a couple of important statistical measures, we can now move on.

SUMMARY

In Chapter 2 we have looked at some basic mathematical ideas and operations that we can now use to do some statistics. Most important among these are the four rules of number together with percentages.

We have also introduced two important statistical measures. These are averages, which are measures of central tendency, and the standard deviation, which is a measure of dispersion.

We are now ready to start using these methods with some real data.

Chapter 3

Organizing and Analyzing Information

As we collect data in real contexts, it soon becomes obvious that we have to deal with much larger sets of numbers and with more complex information than the simple sets and data we used yesterday. We therefore need some techniques to help us sort, classify, organize, and structure large amounts of data.

In looking at these techniques we will consider

- the processing of information.
- the use of spreadsheets.
- spreadsheet business applications.

As you combine individual facts and figures you can organize and process them, and thus they become more useful. You have then transformed the raw data into information. This has a number of advantages. First, it enables you to take in information at a glance—by organizing it you have a better knowledge or picture of it. Second, you have prepared it for the next stage of the statistical process, that of *analysis*. You are now able to operate on the numbers to produce those statistical measures that you need in order to describe important features of the information.

THE PROCESSING OF INFORMATION

Let us now look at the processes we can use to make sense of and order data as it arrives.

Consider the following set of data:

57.20	7.40	48.32	52.69	43.01	20.60
62.13	70.90	81.10	60.15	93.45	76.56
37.41	41.64	51.38	30.80	49.75	21.33
55.72	69.81	32.32	64.36	9.87	48.74
64.35	45.46	47.63	56.54	78.76	89.77
29.38	74.65	58.49	25.14	42.33	38.47
71.28	92.38	3.20	73.46	54.45	50.61
28.17	96.85	53.44	43.35	22.13	63.54
98.97	35.26	67.58	46.37	87.78	44.35
59.49	79.88	24.35	65.56	54.46	75.67

What can we do with this? Well, the first and most obvious thing is that we need to identify what it is. It is surprising how often this simple step gets missed. Any collection of data should be titled to identify it properly. The set of data shown here is the set of cash register totals at a supermarket over a one-hour period.

The time of day when this data was gathered may also be significant, and should normally be included. For our purposes, however, we will not be concerned with this. We are only interested in what we can *do* with the data.

The next step is to look at the values themselves. This data is exactly correct, and is given in cents. For the purposes of analysis, we don't need that level of detail. Therefore we will simplify the data by giving it in dollars. We can't do this by just cutting off the cents, as this would distort the data. We will therefore round the figures to the nearest dollar.

Frequency distributions

The next step is often to arrange the data into a *frequency distribution* or table. This is done when there are values that appear often in a collection of data, and it is frequently carried out by using a table. To do this we simply list the values and mark off each occurrence of that value as we go through the data. Normally we would add a column for the total tally, or frequency (for which we use the letter f). A frequency distribution looks like this:

Variable	Tally	Frequency
11	I	1
12	II	2
13	IIII	4
14	~~IIII~~ I	6
15	~~IIII~~ II	7
16	~~IIII~~	5
17	~~IIII~~	5
18	III	3
19	II	2
20	II	2

In our cash register example, though, many values are unused, and there are no multiple occurrences of the same values, so we will leave out this stage.

Grouping data

For many collections of real data, there is another step that you can perform to simplify things even more. This is to *group* the data. With any set of real data, it is not always obvious how you should group it. This is always a matter of choice. When doing this you should bear in mind the following.

- ◆ Every value should be able to fit into a group.
- ◆ The groups should not overlap; a value should only be able to fit into one group.
- ◆ There should not be too many groups. Between five and 12 is usually the right number to give the balance between simplicity and complexity.
- ◆ It is easier if the groups are the same size.

Here is the cash register data collected into five groups. The group frequency distribution is the most usual way for large collections of data to be presented.

$	Tally	Frequency
0 – 19	III	3
20 – 39	~~IIII~~ ~~IIII~~ II	12
40 – 59	~~IIII~~ ~~IIII~~ ~~IIII~~ ~~IIII~~ II	22
60 – 79	~~IIII~~ ~~IIII~~ ~~IIII~~ I	16
80 – 99	~~IIII~~ II	7

It must be remembered that by grouping we have lost some information—the individual values—in order to gain some simplicity. However, what we now have makes it much easier to view and appreciate the spread of the whole collection of data. The data is also now much easier to analyze.

There are now many things that we can do with this information, and exactly what we do will depend on the application and the requirements. With our supermarket information, we will calculate the mean and the standard deviation, to show how we work with grouped data.

But how can we calculate the mean if we can't add up the individual values? As always in statistics, we do the next best thing. We are going to make an assumption that all of the values in a group have the value of the *mid-point* of that group. With large collections of data, this works out to be pretty accurate, as those values above the mid-point tend to balance out those below.

But what is the mid-point? This can be tricky to calculate. Let us take the group \$20 – \$39. Remember, we added a complication because we rounded the figures. So in our group, the smallest value that comes into the group is \$19.50, and the largest value is \$39.49. For simplicity, let us call the largest figure \$39.50. The difference between these two values is \$39.50 – \$19.50 = \$20. The mid-point will then be \$10 on from the \$19.50, which is \$29.50.

In practice, it is simpler to calculate the mid-point by adding together the lower and upper limits of the group interval and dividing by two. This would give us \$20 + \$39 = \$59. \$59 divided by 2 = \$29.50, which is the same as we calculated before.

Now we can calculate the mean. To do this we multiply the frequency by the mid-point value for each group interval and add them together. This is equivalent to adding up all of the values. Now we divide by the *number* of values. The table and the calculation are shown below.

	Frequency (f)	**Mid-point (x)**	fx
0 – 19	3	9.5	28.5
20 – 39	12	29.5	354.0
40 – 59	22	49.5	1089.0
60 – 79	16	69.5	1112.0
80 – 99	7	89.5	626.5
	$\Sigma f = 60$		$\Sigma fx = 3210$

In symbols, the mean is:

$$\bar{x} = \frac{\Sigma fx}{\Sigma f} = \frac{3210}{60} = 53.5$$

To calculate the standard deviation, perform the following steps.

- **Step 1** For each group, calculate the difference between the mid-point value and the mean.
- **Step 2** Square these values.
- **Step 3** Multiply this by the frequency.
- **Step 4** Total this final column and divide by the total frequency.
- **Step 5** Take the square root.

	f	x	$x-\bar{x}$	$(x-\bar{x})^2$	$f(x-\bar{x})^2$
0 – 19	3	9.5	–44	1936	5808
20 – 39	12	29.5	–24	576	6912
40 – 59	22	49.5	–4	16	352
60 – 79	16	69.5	16	256	4096
80 – 99	7	89.5	36	1296	9072
	$\Sigma f = 60$				$\Sigma f(x-\bar{x})^2 = 26240$

The formula for standard deviation is:

$$s=\sqrt{\frac{\Sigma f\,(x-\bar{x})^2}{\Sigma f}}=\sqrt{\frac{26240}{60}}=20.9$$

Remember that the standard deviation is the average difference of the values from the mean. So on average, each value is $20.90 (higher or lower) away from the mean.

And as before, there is a simplified formula:

$$s=\sqrt{\frac{\Sigma fx^2}{\Sigma f}-\left(\frac{\Sigma fx}{\Sigma f}\right)^2}$$

You may notice that these figures and the calculations can get very large and cumbersome. To avoid this there are shortcut methods to calculate the mean, and these involve choosing an *assumed mean*. This simplifies the calculations. Standard deviation calculations can usually be automated by calculator or computer, which takes the drudgery out of the large numbers.

Of course, there are other procedures that can be used to help order and simplify large amounts of data. But the use of frequency distributions and grouping is by far the most common and most powerful.

THE USE OF SPREADSHEETS

For many large collections of real data, computer spreadsheets are used to collect, organize, and analyze the information. This is particularly true of financial information, but spreadsheets can also be used for any kind of numerical data, like production figures, and so on. The value of the spreadsheet is that once the data is entered it can be manipulated very quickly in many very sophisticated ways. This means the analysis (and the arithmetic) is automated. In order to do this, of course, you need a reasonable level of computer literacy and you need to learn one of the spreadsheet

programs available. Perhaps one of the most used commercial spreadsheet programs is Lotus 1-2-3, but there are many good alternative programs. We introduce the idea here to illustrate what can be done, the terminology, and the possibilities.

Most people in business and commercial contexts are being asked to read information from spreadsheets. What follows should serve as an introduction to the basic functions of a spreadsheet. A more detailed coverage of spreadsheet usage can be obtained from books, or from actually using a program.

Although all spreadsheet programs vary slightly, the basic principles of operation are the same. A spreadsheet involves a grid like the one shown here.

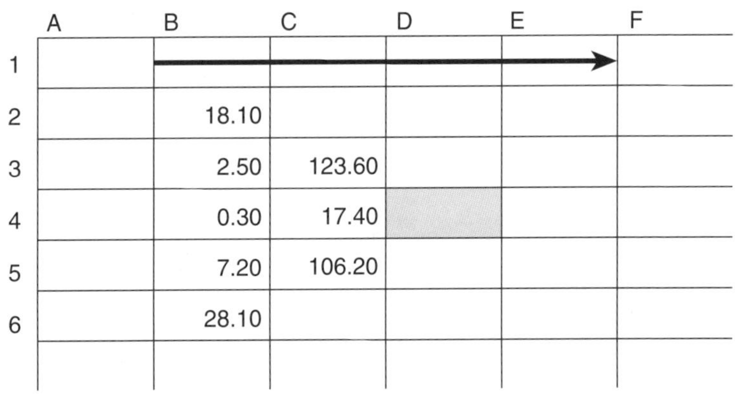

A cell is a space in the grid, and is named by its row and column location. Here, the shaded cell is D4. You can enter data into any of the cells as text or as a number. Rows and columns are denoted by the addresses of the cells that make it up. In the diagram, the line represents the row B1:E1.

Once you have your data in the spreadsheet, you can manipulate it and use it to perform a huge range of operations and calculations. In fact, you can use almost any combination of mathematical functions, logical functions, and functions provided within the program itself. This you do by putting a formula into a cell. For instance, you can find the difference between the values in cells C3 and C4 and place the answer in cell C5. You do this by moving to cell C5 (by using the cursor/arrow keys) and entering the formula:

C3 – C4

You may need to instruct the spreadsheet to recalculate.

You can do row or column totals by using the sum function. If you move to cell B6 and enter the formula:

SUM B2:B5

it will add up the values in the cells B2, B3, B4, and B5, and place the answer in cell B6 as shown.

Moreover, if you want to add all of the column totals from C2:C5 to M2:M5 (maybe sales totals for each month in a year), instead of typing out the column-total formula 12 times, you can use the *replicate* (or *copy*) function.

The syntax and terminology of these commands may vary slightly from one program to another, but they all have a very similar range of functions. We can show some of the possibilities by using a simple example. A typical budget is shown in the table on page 37.

You should be able to add up the income costs for the year by summing the row in which they appear. You can find the direct costs for April by summing the design and print costs. And now you can use the replicate function to find the sum for the other months. The gross profit is found by subtracting the total direct costs from the income, for each month.

You can then finish off the other totals by

- summing the overhead figures to get a total for each month.
- calculating the *net profit* by subtracting the total overheads from the gross profit for each month.
- calculating the *cumulative profit* by taking the cumulative profit for the previous month and adding the net profit for the current month.

Once you have these totals you can calculate some useful statistics. The *net margin* is found by dividing the net profit by the income and multiplying by 100 to express it as a percentage. You can also calculate the mean (average) monthly income.

The spreadsheet can also be used to ask "What if?" type questions. For instance, you can assess the impact of adding another sales executive to your staff by increasing the staff figure and making a guess or estimate as to the increase in sales.

SPREADSHEET BUSINESS APPLICATIONS

The example on page 37 shows how you might use a spreadsheet to organize and analyze a fairly routine budget. However, the same principles and software can also be applied to an enormous range of business-related facts and figures. Here are a few of the many possibilities:

- project estimating
- departmental budgets with actuals and variances
- cash flow statements
- price schedules
- maintenance schedules

	Apr	May	Jun	Jul	Aug	Sep	Oct	Nov	Dec	Jan	Feb	Mar	Year
Income	39,350	29,250	21,100	50,700	10,800	76,050	63,400	71,100	51,150	40,000	–	47,210	
Direct costs													
Design	4,200	2,700	2,100	5,800	1,100	3,250	8,050	6,800	5,300	4,500	5,150	1,300	
Print	14,600	8,200	9,200	18,600	4,000	34,800	21,900	28,100	18,910	16,400	17,200	3,200	
Total													
Gross Profit													
Overheads													
Staff	13,800	13,800	13,800	13,800	13,800	13,800	13,800	15,200	15,200	15,200	15,200	15,200	
Rent	1,050	1,050	1,050	1,050	1,050	1,050	1,050	1,050	1,050	1,050	1,050	1,050	
Office													
Stationery	20	–	–	160	–	80	–	210	–	–	60	–	
Mail	120	90	30	180	210	50	80	110	40	60	160	90	
Telephone	–	–	480	–	–	520	–	–	450	–	–	510	
Photocopy	60	15	40	–	75	–	90	–	35	–	55	–	
Travel													
Lease	180	180	180	180	180	180	180	180	180	180	180	180	
Gas/Oil	65	20	32	80	40	60	55	28	35	65	40	30	
Insurance	–	350	–	–	–	–	–	–	–	–	–	–	
Rail/Air	210	22	–	320	–	90	66	–	42	160	–	280	
Finance/accounts	250	250	250	250	250	250	250	250	250	250	250	250	
Miscellaneous	280	130	210	300	165	220	350	95	240	185	135	235	
Total overheads													
Net profit													
Cumulative profit													

In any application, the value of the information depends on two factors. The first is the quality of the information. This involves collecting the right information and ensuring its accuracy and reliability. The second factor (which is interdependent with the first) is the type of questions you need to ask. This is often ignored, and people often collect information without regard to what they might need to use it for. A huge proportion of information in most organizations is wasted and unused, because no one gives thought to what its purpose or function might be.

People should start with the questions and then determine what information is worth collecting. This approach requires not statistical skills but common sense and business experience. Take the example of a sales manager with a large team of salespeople operating nationwide. What kind of questions might need to be asked?

- What is the budget for actual sales or costs?
- What are the expenses and sales generated by each salesperson?
- What proportion of sales comes from new customers?

The idea occurs to this sales manager that there are certain ratios that will give an indication of the productivity and efficiency of the area of operation. In this case, ratios might include

- sales per salesperson.
- sales per dollar of expenses.
- sales breakdown by product.

Such performance measures are important in any area of business or commercial life. Examples include

- sales per employee.
- profit per employee.
- costs per employee.

These apply in the public sector and the not-for-profit sector as much as anywhere else. Examples of ratios include

Services:

- net cost per 1,000 population
- staff per 1,000 population

Education:

- pupil:teacher ratio
- cost per pupil

Social work:

- staff per 1,000 population

Police:

- crimes per 1,000 population

Highways:

- maintenance cost per mile

SUMMARY

We have looked at the techniques used to organize and analyze large collections of data—these include the use of frequency distributions and the technique of grouping data. We have shown how to calculate the mean and standard deviation for grouped data. And finally, we have examined how spreadsheets can be used to organize and analyze data, as well as some of the uses that they can make of information. Now we are ready to show how to illustrate data.

Chapter 4

Illustrating Data

One of the most useful and powerful things you can do with data once it is collected and organized is to illustrate it. Pictures are easier to interpret than columns of figures, and illustrating data helps you take in the totality of the data at a glance. In many cases this is worth a good deal of analysis in itself.

In this chapter, we will look at the most important and well-used techniques for illustrating data. However, it should be noted that there are a large number of methods and literally hundreds of variations, and an element of creativity is called for. These techniques will give you a start, but you need to use them according to the context, and even, on occasion, to invent your own variants of them.

The techniques we will look at include the following.

- pictograms and ideagrams
- bar charts
- pie charts
- illustrating frequency distributions

PICTOGRAMS AND IDEAGRAMS

These are possibly the simplest type of diagram with which to illustrate data. In *pictograms* some form of picture or icon is used to represent the data.

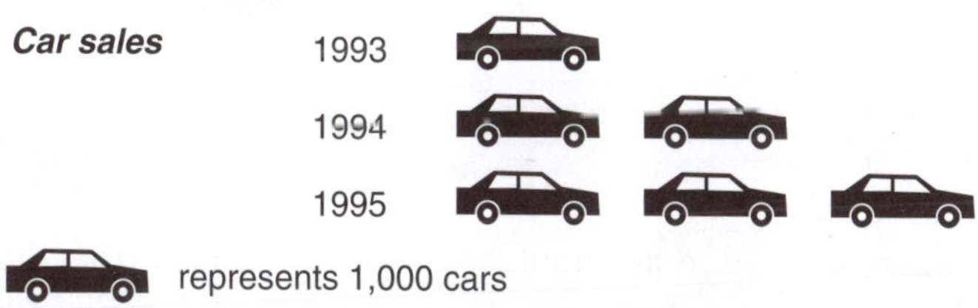

The number of repetitions of the icon represents the frequency, but you need to decide on a suitable scale, and this should be shown with the diagram.

The advantage of pictograms is that they are very sharp visually and explicit, and need little verbal or numerical explanation. Their disadvantage is they are inaccurate and you lose the exact value of the variables.

A variation on the pictogram is the *ideagram*. This is where it is not the number of icons that represents the frequency or value but some other aspect of the picture instead. Ideagrams can be quite creative, and there are endless possible variations.

With *statistical maps*, the map itself gives location, while graphic embellishments like shading, dots, or the size of arrows or other features give visual information about the values of the variable. Such maps can be difficult to scale, however, and it is not always easy to read detailed values.

BAR CHARTS

Bar charts are used to illustrate measurements of data from different times or at different places. The principle is that the length of the bar represents the value of the factor being measured. Thus, it is important to have a scale of some sort. Bar charts are very easy to draw and equally easy to understand.

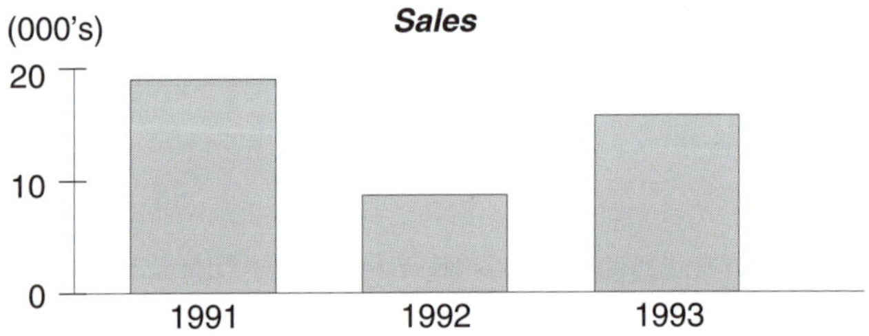

However, they can be limited in power as they are restricted to showing differences in only one factor, though they can be made more powerful by using one of a number of variations, which include:

Component bar charts, where each value is broken down into its component parts:

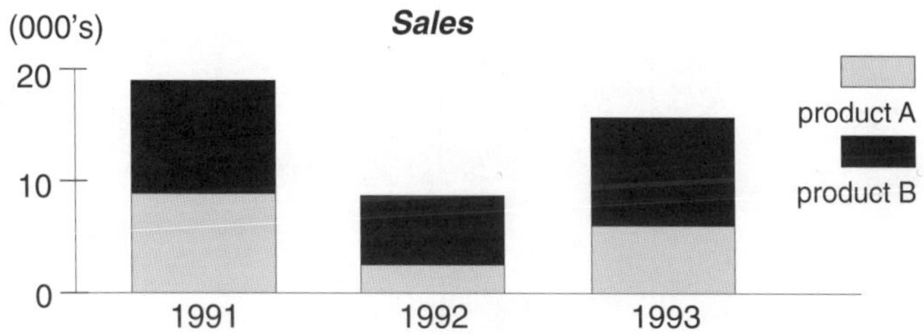

Percentage bar charts, where the components are broken down into percentage parts, each bar representing 100 percent of some factor:

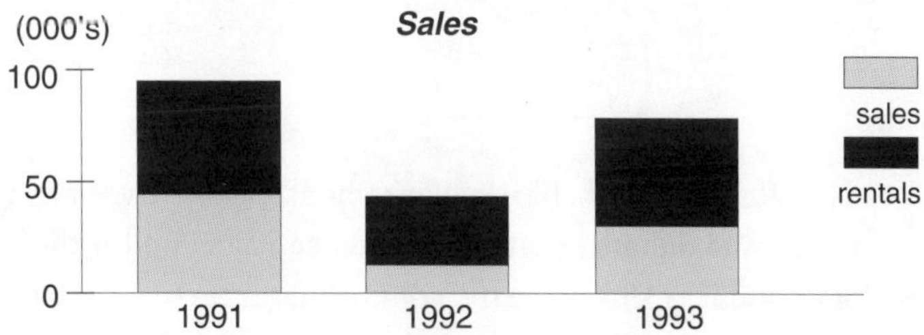

Multiple bar charts, which can be effective in comparing sets of data:

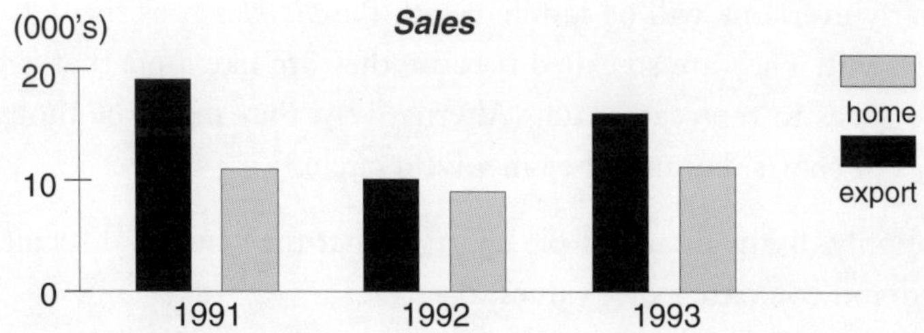

Block diagrams, which are like a single bar of a component bar chart:

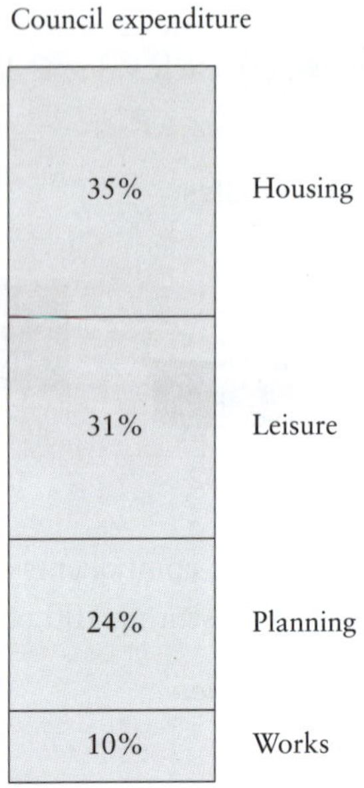

The only difference with block diagrams is that if they are two dimensional, it is the area that represents the value; and if they are three dimensional, it should be the volume that represents the value. The possibility for misinterpretation is discussed in Chapter 7.

PIE CHARTS

Nearly everyone will be familiar with the *pie chart*, as they are so prevalent. They are so called because they are like a pie that is cut into slices to represent data. (Alternatively, they might be thought of as **pi** charts, because they involve a circle.)

The only disadvantage of pie charts is that they can be difficult to read and compare exact values.

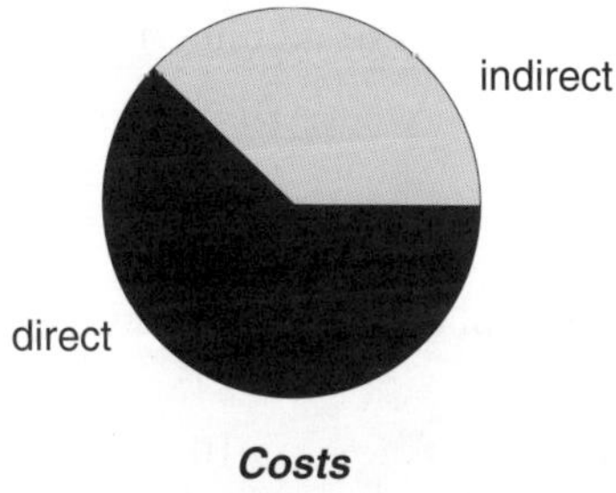

Here is how to construct a pie chart with a set of figures. Basically, it is the angle at the center of the circle that represents the value. So if you were illustrating a single factor with a total value of 360 (e.g., \$360), each \$1 of value would be represented by 1°. However, if you were illustrating a factor with a total value of 180, each unit would be represented by 360/180 or 2°.

Let's illustrate a slightly more complicated example with some real figures.

Sources of admin errors

Error	Frequency	Angle (degrees)
Typing	84	84 × 1.8° = 151.2
Filing	43	77.4
Wrong telephone number	34	61.2
Incomplete document	21	37.8
Not in diary	10	18.0
Lost document	5	9.0
Other	3	5.4
	200	360.0

STEP 1

To illustrate this set of figures, first find the total. This is 200 errors.

STEP 2

Now calculate the angle for a single unit. This is 360 divided by the total. 360 ÷ 200 = 1.8°.

STEP 3

Now find the size of the segment for each component by multiplying the value by the angle per unit calculated in Step 2.

The results are shown in the table.

STEP 4

With a protractor, start to measure the angles, starting from a single radius line.

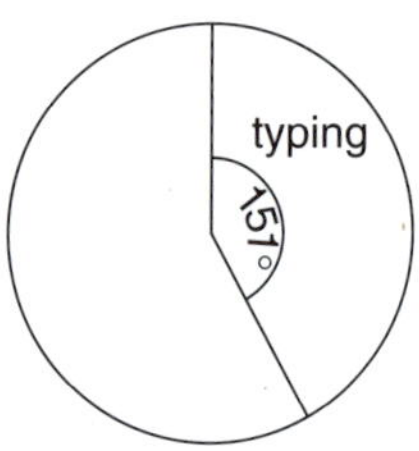

Costs

ILLUSTRATING FREQUENCY DISTRIBUTIONS

The most common method used to illustrate a frequency distribution is the *histogram*. People often assume that a histogram is just a technical term for a bar chart. In fact they are quite different. With ungrouped data, they do look like bar charts. But in a histogram it is the area of the bar that represents the value, not just the height. This becomes significant with grouped data, although if the class intervals are the same, then the heights of the bars can be compared.

Here is the example we used in Chapter 2.

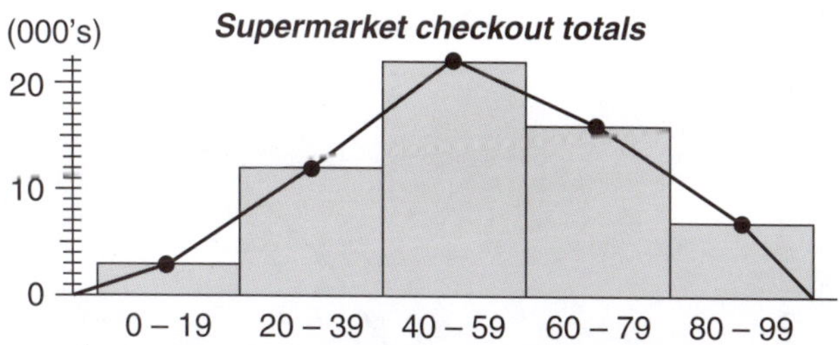

Histograms are good at representing the shape of a distribution, if the intervals have been chosen well. The distribution can also be represented by a *frequency polygon*, constructed by joining the mid-points of each interval with a straight line. This has been done in the supermarket checkout diagram. You may notice that the line is finished off at each end, so that the area under the curve represents the total distribution.

Another line that is often drawn with single variables is the cumulative frequency. This is obtained by totaling the values to date. We will see a use for the cumulative frequency in Chapter 5.

The table "Weights of a sample population" shows a simple frequency distribution, with the cumulative frequencies added. The cumulative frequency is then shown in the next illustration.

Weights of a sample population

Weight (kg)	Frequency	Cumulative Frequency
60.5 – 62.5	1	1
62.5 – 64.5	6	7
64.5 – 66.5	11	18
66.5 – 68.5	15	33
68.5 – 70.5	10	43
70.5 – 72.5	5	48
72.5 – 74.5	2	50

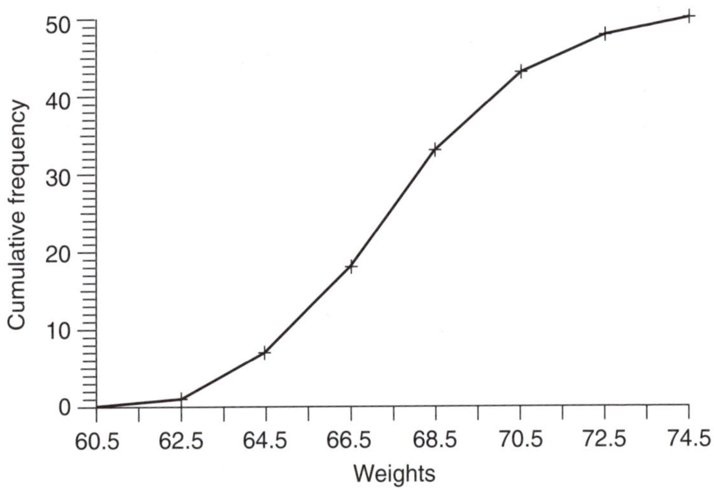

Spreadsheet graphics

Most of the industry standard computer spreadsheet packages referred to in Chapter 3 have graphics packages attached to them. This means that they will take the information from a spreadsheet, illustrate it in a statistical diagram of your choice, and print it out. The calculation is automated; they are very easy to use and they produce professional and powerful results.

Shape of distributions

As you become familiar with illustrations of frequency distributions, you will see that they can take many shapes and forms. Some distributions are asymmetrical, like these:

In statistics, this asymmetry, or skewness, can be described and measured. Some distributions are short and fat, and some are tall and thin. This property, called *kurtosis*, can also be described and measured.

However, you may notice that there is one characteristic shape that recurs. The diagram on page 52 shows how a frequency distribution with more groups and more data approaches this ideal shape.

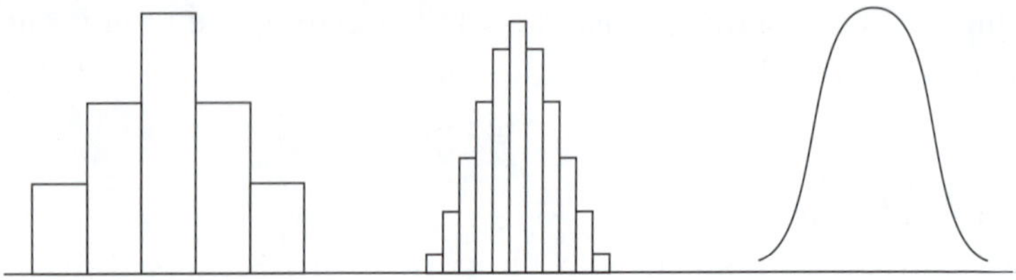

This shape is called a normal curve, and variations on this shape of distribution appear for many natural quantities—particularly where people are involved. Because of its prevalence in the natural world, there is a great deal of math that describes and analyzes various aspects of such distributions. To give you some examples, we know that:

68% of the distribution lies within one standard deviation of the mean

95% of the distribution lies within two standard deviations of the mean

Such facts become very useful for advanced statistics.

SUMMARY

In Chapter 4 we have explored some of the most important methods for illustrating data. These include pictograms, bar charts, and pie charts, and their variations. We have shown how a histogram can be used to illustrate a frequency distribution, and how to add on a cumulative frequency curve. Good spreadsheets have graphics packages that will produce these pictures automatically from a set of data. Finally, we have discussed shapes of curves, and the importance of the normal curve. We now move on from diagrams to look at graphs and charts.

Chapter 5

Just in Time

In this chapter, we will look at the illustration of data using graphs and charts of various sorts, but particularly at quantities that vary in relation to time. We will look at

- time series.
- Gannt charts.
- straight line graphs.
- scatter diagrams (and correlation).

TIME SERIES

Time series are cases in which we graph some quantity or factor against a time scale. In such cases we are interested in knowing how certain variables vary over time. Typical among these variables are

- demand.
- costs.
- sales.
- consumer or market trends.

By illustrating such data on a graph, we can get an immediate picture of the variation over time. On analysis, we may also be able to spot trends, seasonal variations, and random variations.

The figures in the following table would be a fairly typical set of data to plot on a time series graph.

Quarterly sales figures ($000's)

	Q1	Q2	Q3	Q4
1993	27	47	58	39
1994	33	56	82	46
1995	47	74	94	62

You can see that there are patterns in the rise and fall of these figures. Sales increase towards the third quarter, and then drop off in the fourth quarter. This is the seasonal variation. By examining the quarterly sales figures graph you may also notice a tendency for the figures to rise over the period. Such a long-term rise or fall is called the *trend*. The method for identifying trends is called the *moving average*. This is a set of averages (means) taken at each stage along the time axis. For monthly figures, for instance, it would be normal to take an average for 12 months. The reason it is called moving is because the values that are averaged move along one period at a time. In our example, the averages are: Q1 to Q4 of 1993; Q2 to Q4 of 1993 plus Q1 of 1994; Q3 to Q4 of 1993 plus Q1 to Q2 of 1994; and so on. Here we show the table with the moving averages calculated, and on page 56, we show the graph of the data, with the moving averages also plotted.

	1993				1994				1995			
	Q1	Q2	Q3	Q4	Q1	Q2	Q3	Q4	Q1	Q2	Q3	Q4
Sales ($000's)	27	47	58	39	33	56	82	46	47	74	94	62
Moving average		42.75	44.25	46.50	52.50	54.25	57.75	62.25	65.25	69.25		

The average is a four-quarterly average, and it is plotted in the middle of the period. Once it has been plotted we can *extrapolate* from the trend. We do this by continuing the line (shown dotted on our graph). From this we can make predictions about the future. Of course, there are also inherent dangers in doing this, and care must be taken not to rely too much on such predictions.

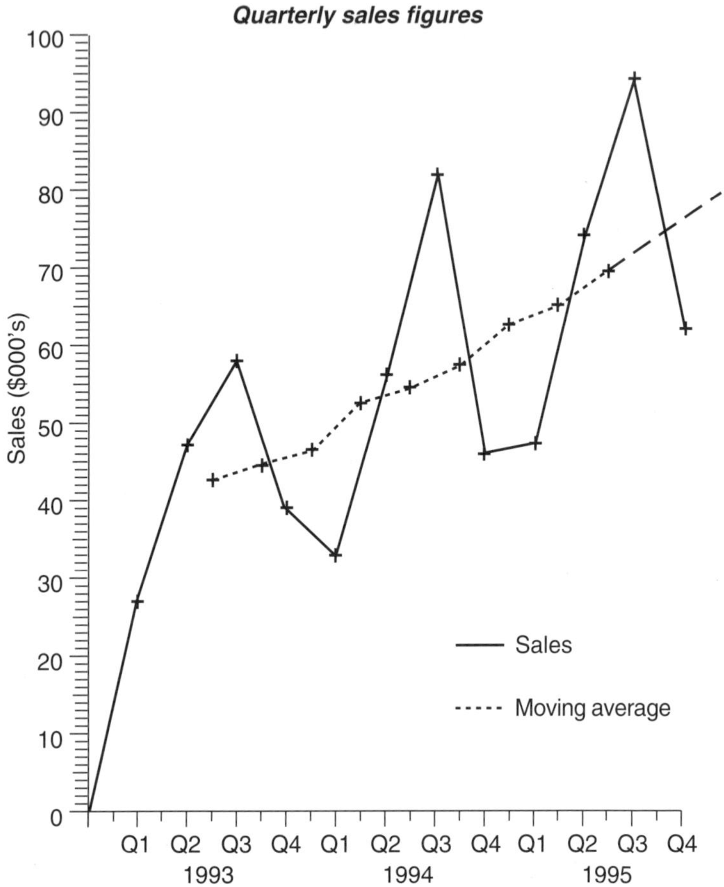

It is possible to adjust for seasonal variations by examining the differences relative to the trend. Other major variations in a time series graph are called *random variations*. Once these have been identified (by eliminating the trend and the seasonal variations), they can be examined in more detail. Of course, they often turn out to be anything but random. Once identified, the potential causes can be isolated and checked.

GANNT CHARTS

An interesting variation on the notion of plotting quantities against time is the *Gannt chart*. You may be familiar with Gannt charts from a project management point of view, but in business statistics, they have a particular use. This is in mapping actual against planned performance on a time line.

Let us look at the example of sales targets broken down into monthly figures. The targets, and the actual sales achieved, are shown in this table.

Month	Target ($000's)	Actual ($000's)
Jan	6	5.5
Feb	6	7.0
March	6	6.0
April	8	8.5
May	8	9.0
June	10	10.5
	44	46.5

And they are mapped as follows.

- **Step 1** Draw the time line, and add in the planned (budgeted) and actual amounts.
- **Step 2** Calculate the actual amount as a percentage of the budgeted amount. This is done by dividing actual by budget and multiplying by a hundred.

- **Step 3** Draw a bar to represent this percentage on the Gannt chart, using the *time scale* for the month to represent 100 percent. Thus, the line may fall short of the budgeted amount, in which case it leaves a gap, or it may exceed it, in which case the extra component is drawn underneath, as shown for February on the diagram.

- **Step 4** Draw in the cumulative total, using the same scale. This total will show whether the year to date is above or below target. In the case of the figures illustrated, the final cumulative total is *above* budget.

	Jan	Feb	Mar	April	May	June	
Target	6.0	6.0	6.0	8.0	8.0	10.0	
Actual	5.5	7.0	6.0	8.5	9.0	10.5	
%	91.7	117.0	100.0	106.3	112.5	105.0	

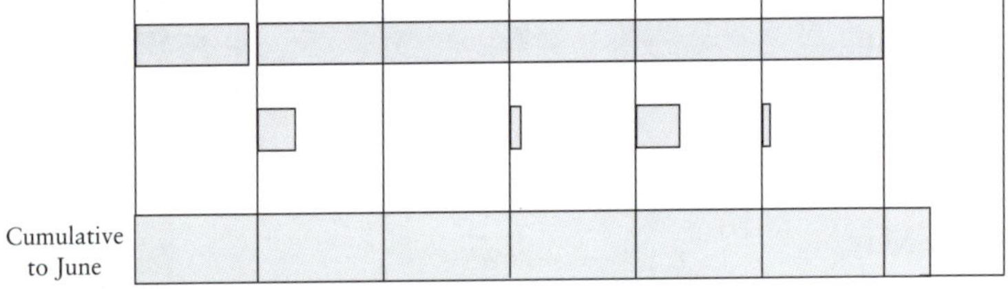

STRAIGHT LINE GRAPHS

Where two quantities are plotted against each other, there are many applications where time is not one of the quantities. Further, sometimes the two quantities are in a linear relationship to each other. This means that, when the values are plotted on a graph, the result is a straight line. We will show one way in which such a graph might be used.

Take the following example. In many production contexts, costs are made up of two basic components:

The *variable costs* vary strictly according to the number of units processed or manufactured, and usually include labor and material costs. For simplicity's sake, let us say that each single unit costs $5 to produce. In this case 10 units would cost 10 × $5 = $50, and 100 units would cost 100 × $5 = $500, and so on.

The *fixed costs*, or the overheads, are those costs that would always be incurred however many units were manufactured or sold. These include salaries, rents, office costs, and so on. Let us say that the fixed costs are $10,000. We can calculate the revenue, because we know that each unit is sold at, say, $10.

In a *break-even chart*, we show the sales revenue and the costs, in relation to different levels of sales, on the same graph. Each will be a straight line. Let us plot each line separately.

First the revenue line. We estimate that we might sell as many as 5,000 units in a year. One of the advantages of straight lines is that we only need two points to join up in order to draw the line. If we sell no units, the revenue is \$0. If we sell 5,000 units, the revenue is 5,000 × \$10 = \$50,000.

Now we draw the axes on the graph. Notice on the graph below that we have used whole numbers (of thousands) for both units and dollars, to simplify the graph. Our two points have the coordinates (0, 0) and (5, 50). We now plot these and join them to make the revenue line.

To plot the cost line, we need to calculate both the fixed and variable components of the cost. We will do the calculation for *three* values (just as a check that they are all on the same straight line).

No. of units (1,000's)	Fixed cost (\$1,000)	Variable cost (\$1,000)	Total cost (\$1,000)
0	10	0 × 5 = 0	10
1	10	1 × 5 = 5	15
5	10	5 × 5 = 25	35

The pairs of values (number of units, total cost of units) are: (0, 10) (1, 15) (5, 35). These can now be plotted on the graph.

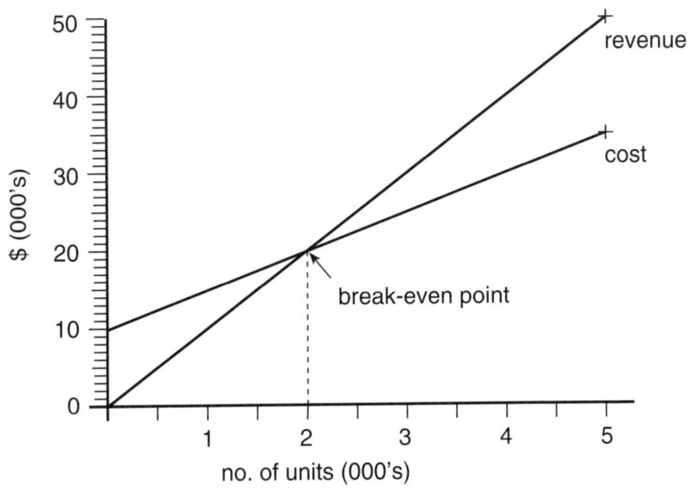

It should be easy to see that below where they cross, the costs are higher than the revenue, and so we operate at a loss. Above (to the right of) that point, the revenues are higher than the costs, and so we are operating at a profit. The point where they cross is called the *break-even point,* and it represents the number of units that we have to sell in order to break even. This is 2,000 units, as shown on the graph.

SCATTER DIAGRAMS

Some quantities, when plotted against each other, show a relationship between the variables involved. Such relationships are *not* necessarily straight lines, like those in the example on page 59. In order to find out more about the nature of such relationships you can plot pairs of values of the two variables on a graph called a *scatter diagram*. This will give you a visual idea of how they might be related, and how close that relationship is.

Various patterns of relationships between variables are shown in the diagrams on the next page.

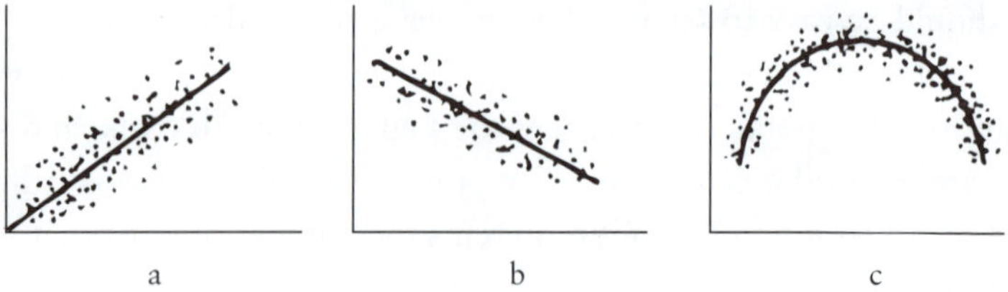

When the scatter diagram has given you an idea about the correlation between the variables you can then use more analytic methods for describing the relationship involved. However, for many purposes the graphic information is enough to tell you what you need to know.

SUMMARY

In Chapter 5 we have looked at how graphs and charts can be used to illustrate certain kinds of data.

Time series are a way to plot a variable against time. We can use this to analyze trends and seasonal variations. Gannt charts are a way of measuring performance against a time frame. When variables are plotted against each other, they can have a straight line or linear relationship. We can use straight line graphs to do calculations such as break-even analysis. When we are unsure about the relationship between variables, we use a scatter diagram to illustrate that relationship.

Chapter 6

Methods and Techniques

Having set out the basic ideas and techniques of statistics, we now move on to present an overview of more advanced ideas and tools. Space does not permit us to give a detailed account of the mechanics of these often very complex and abstract ideas, but in reading this section, you will see what kind of ideas and tools are available. This is one step on the way to appreciating the impact they have on your business life. The next step might be to follow up with a more specialized or advanced book and learn in more detail.

This chapter covers

- an introduction to probability.

- statistical methods summation.
- lies, damned lies, and statistics.

INTRODUCTION TO PROBABILITY

Many of the more advanced ideas in statistics involve use of the concept of *probability*. Probability is important in statistics for two main reasons: so much of the real world of business is surrounded by inherent uncertainty, and probability is a mathematical way of trying to deal with that uncertainty.

In statistics in general, probability is important because many statistical techniques are based on the aforementioned notion of *sampling*. When we take a statistical sample from any population we need to bear in mind the confidence with which we can assume that the sample represents the parent population. So much of the influence of probability is around the level of confidence in the conclusions and statements made.

Probability begins with some very simple ideas. The probability of a particular outcome happening is the ratio of the number of times it can happen to the total number of possible outcomes. So if we have three green balls and two red balls in a bag, the probability of a green ball being pulled out at random is:

$$\frac{\text{number of favorable outcomes}}{\text{total number of outcomes}} = \frac{3}{5}$$

All probabilities are expressed as fractions (or more usually decimals) between zero and one.

Things get a bit more complicated when we start to consider more than one event. With multiple events, we need to look at all of the possible outcomes, and this can be done either by listing them or illustrating them on a probability space diagram. For example, with two flips of a coin, the outcome has to be one of the following:

HH
HT
TT
TH

From this it can be seen that with two flips of a coin, the probability that there is exactly one head is 2/4, or a half, or 0.5. The number of outcomes with one head is two (TH HT), and the total number of outcomes is 4.

If we look at the outcomes for three flips of a coin, we get:

0 heads	1 head	2 heads	3 heads
1	3	3	1

If we carry on this process with four flips, five flips, and so on, we get a pattern of figures called Pascal's Triangle, as illustrated on page 67.

1

1 1

1 2 1

1 3 3 1

1 4 6 4 1

1 5 10 10 5 1

1 6 15 20 15 6 1

If you take successive rows of this triangle and plot them as histograms, they become increasingly like this:

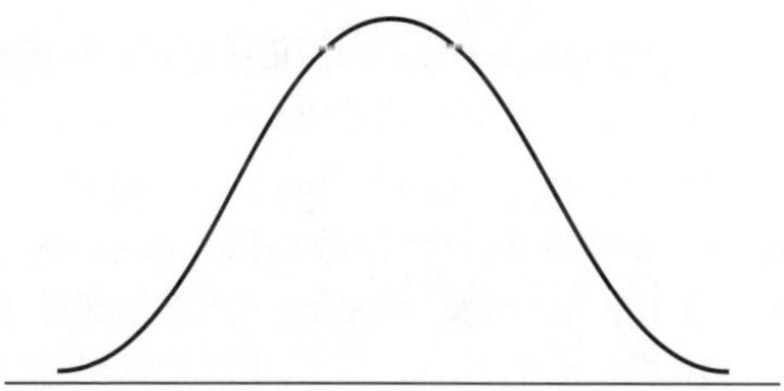

This probability distribution is very like the distributions we see with such quantities, and this enables us to make certain kinds of predictions and calculations about such quantities. For instance, we can predict the probability of a person selected at random being within a particular height range.

We can use probabilities to test certain kinds of statements, called hypotheses. Look at the test scores given in the table:

Percentage of pupils achieving levels at Key Stage 3, 1994, for English

	Levels									
	1	2	3	4	5	6	7	8	9	10
School	0	1	2	16	34	35	7	3	1	1
National	1	3	10	23	27	22	8	1	0	0

The school scores seem to be better than the national average. But how can we be *sure* that the school is performing better than the national average? How can we be sure that the differences are not just random or natural variation? We could of course calculate some summative statistics, and we may then find that the average level achieved for the school *is* indeed higher than the national average. We need some kind of statistical method, using the ideas of probability, that can answer such questions.

Other examples might involve the use of statistical methods to control production processes. Consider the example of sampling bags of sugar from a filling machine. The bags should be 5 lb. in weight and cannot be sold with a weight lower than that. Because the bags vary, you may set the average weight of fill higher than 5 lb. to

ensure that the bags will weigh at least 5 lb. The problem for the producer is that if the average is set too high, sugar is given away, but if the average is set too low, some bags may be underfilled.

There are two ways that the filling process can go out of control.

1. The average level of fill may go up or down.
2. Even if the average maintains, the variation in fill levels might increase, causing some bags to be underweight.

For the statistician, the challenge is to estimate through sampling what the average weight, the variability, and the likelihood of bags being underweight or overweight are. And because the results come from sampling, it is important to establish with what level of confidence one can say that these statistics are correct.

Setting up control processes for such applications shows the power and importance of probability and statistics.

STATISTICAL METHODS SUMMATION

In this section we will give a summary of methods available within statistics that might be applied in a business context.

Summative statistics

These are the simple calculations, used to describe the main features of a set of data, that yield values for central tendency (averages) and for variation (standard deviation or range). Such calculations can give a feel for the data, and can enable you to predict the results of more complex tests.

Summative statistics also includes measures for skewness and kurtosis, which enable testing for the normality of a set of data.

Most of this book has been about summative statistics.

Single variable statistics

Tests such as the student's t-test can be used to compare data from different sets of circumstances and to test the significance of differences. This approach is also used to test hypotheses, particularly when small samples are used.

Bivariate statistics

This involves tests of the strength and nature of the relationship between two variables. An example might be to establish if there is a direct relationship between sales returns and advertising expenditures. If the relationship is a straight line, it is called *regression analysis*. Scatter diagrams are also used to identify relationships between two variables.

Multivariate statistics

There are methods for dealing with large numbers of variables. *Linear programming* is used to optimize the use of resources and production capability.

Nonparametric statistics

This approach is used when you are unable to make any assumptions about the nature of the data—for instance, that the distribution is normal. The approach includes Spearman's coefficient of rank correlation, where the correlation between two variables is done on the basis of rank orders.

Computerized statistics packages

There exist a number of software packages that contain the full range of statistical tests and tools. These tests are quite automated; all you need to do is type in the data and choose the correct options for the full analysis to be done.

These packages are extremely comprehensive and exhaustive, and are a great boon for those who have more confidence in reading and interpreting results than in performing the mechanical calculations. Also, for busy business executives and managers, the drudgery is taken out of the number crunching, and you can spend your time where it counts—examining the results.

Two examples of statistical software packages are Minitab and SPSS.

LIES, DAMNED LIES, AND STATISTICS

Up to now in this book, we have looked at the techniques of statistics that are appropriate to apply in a business context. But our overview of statistics would not be complete, and you would not be a numerate consumer of statistics, without examining the ways in which statistics are used or misused in other contexts.

We are bombarded by statistics in almost every aspect of our everyday lives:

- in reports and presentations at work
- in newspapers and journals
- in shops and on television

The way that these statistics are prepared and presented is not always done by professionals and, moreover, can be done with a vested interest in mind. You only need to think of the differing interpretations available after an election, all backed up by objective-sounding statistics, to know how people use figures to add authority and objectivity to their arguments.

We will look at some major pitfalls of using statistics and some ways in which statistics are poorly used in the public domain. It will not be difficult for you to find examples of any of these for yourself.

Graphic misrepresentation

Here are the assets of a (fictitious) financial company over a number of years:

Assets, January ($m)

1991	1992	1993	1994	1995	1996
400	440	500	550	500	520

However, what the company chooses to advertise is:

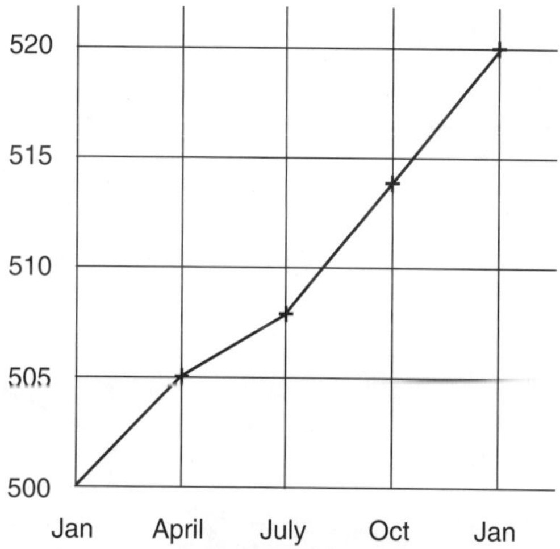

Assets ($m) 1995 – 6

There are two problems here. The first is that the timescale is chosen to flatter the figures. The other problem is that the vertical axis showing the assets does not begin at zero. If it did, the growth of assets would not look at all so spectacular. Any graph or chart where either the horizontal or the vertical axis is compressed or incomplete is going to visually distort the impression you get of the figures. Another way to distort impressions visually is to purposefully confuse length and area in a diagram. Where quantities are being compared using two-dimensional diagrams, you need to examine the scale carefully. Sometimes a doubling of the quantity is shown by a doubling of the dimensions of the diagram. But what the eye sees is the area, and while the dimensions have doubled, the area has *quadrupled*. Such confusion could result from viewing this suitcase diagram.

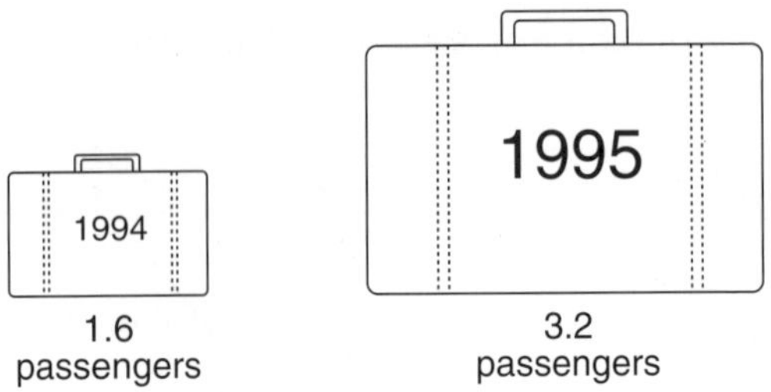

Another visual sleight of hand is to confuse cumulative frequency with just frequency.

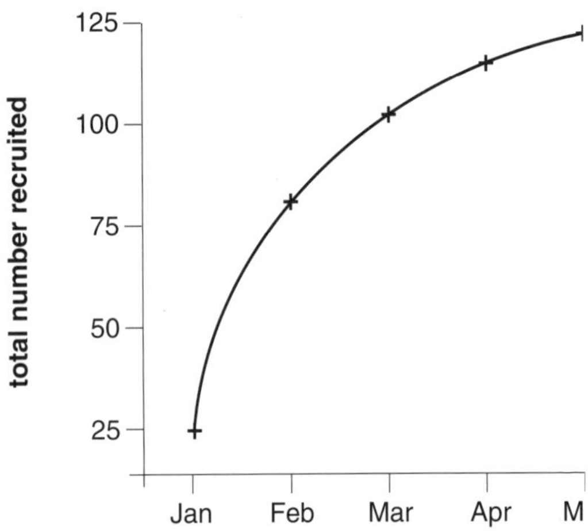

In this diagram, you might be forgiven for thinking that these are the numbers of people being recruited each month. In fact they are the totals to date. If you unscramble the figures, you will see that actually fewer and fewer people are being recruited each month: recruitment is actually *falling*.

Junk logic

There are many many ways to draw incorrect or inappropriate conclusions from a set of data or statistics. Here are a few old favorites.

Cause and effect is a common one. Because you are able to find some relationship between two variables (a correlation), it does not mean that one causes the other. It is said that someone once found a very strong correlation between live births in Australia and the sightings of storks!

More seriously, in the search for cures for diseases, correlations are often found, and they can give clues to causal mechanisms. However, these then have to be tested and verified separately. The two facts that people watch more television and that violence has increased does not mean that television is the *cause* of the increase in violence.

Another way to draw inappropriate conclusions is to examine figures over a period of time without paying attention to *proportions*. When raw figures for a population change—such as the number of people unemployed, or the number of doctors committing suicide—the figures need to be related to the changing numbers for the *total* population. It is possible for such raw figures to increase, but for the proportion in relation to the total population to *decrease*. In such cases, it is the *rate* factor that is of interest.

Rates always have the potential to be confusing. If you read a statement such as "The rate of increase of inflation has slowed down," it can sound rather reassuring. However, inflation is about increases in prices over time, and according to this statement, not only are prices still increasing (even if inflation is falling), but inflation also is still increasing—just not increasing as fast as previously.

Another source of confusion involves using *words* to describe numbers or statistics. It is inevitable that we do this, but great care should be taken when we do. If we express proportions as figures they are unambiguous. However, 51 percent, for example, can be described as *most*, *many* or *more* (more than what?). Once we start using words, the statistics are open to misrepresentation.

The same applies to probability.

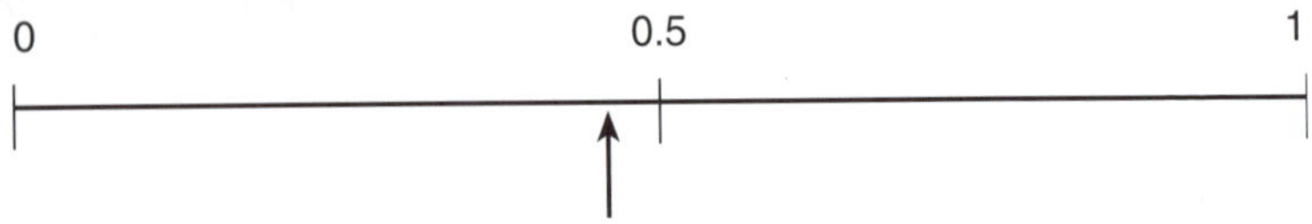

What words would you use to describe the probability marked by the arrow? Depending on how you wanted to argue, you might call it *possibly*, *probably*, *likely* or *unlikely*. Each gives a different imprecision of the same number.

SUMMARY

In Chapter 6 we have tried to complete the picture of business statistics by providing an overview of the tools and techniques available.

We have talked about probability and its importance in many business contexts.

We have summarized and described the kinds of tools and techniques available in our statistical methods summation.

Finally, we have shown some ways that you, as a consumer of statistics, can be misled, to help you to become an intelligent and discriminating consumer of statistics.

In our final chapter we will look at some more advanced techniques that can be applied in business contexts.

Chapter 7

Applications of Business Statistics

So far in this book, we have presented and related basic methods to practical business contexts. We have also explained how more advanced or sophisticated techniques might apply. In this chapter, we cover a selected few techniques that have particular relevance or use in business contexts.

We will cover

- problem solving.
- decision making.
- an index of terms and methods.

PROBLEM SOLVING

In business we are often faced with situations where things are less than ideal. This may arise from some major disturbance or, more likely, from accumulations of minor problems. In such circumstances, it is often difficult to know what is going on, and even more difficult to know what to tackle first.

Pareto analysis is a method for prioritizing problems for solution, and for isolating the most important factors in a problem. It is based on the so-called Pareto Principle, often known as the 80:20 rule.

- 80 percent of sales come from 20 percent of customers
- 80 percent of stock value is tied up in 20 percent of the parts

Pareto analysis is a statistical method of identifying the 20 percent factor that will make the 80 percent difference.

Let us take a very simplified sales-based example to illustrate the Pareto method.

A sales manager suspects that sales staff are spending a disproportionate amount of time with very small accounts that do not deliver profit. The first stage in this kind of problem solving situation is to identify which customers are delivering the bulk of the turnover or profit.

The figures show the sales contributed by each of the listed customers:

Sales ($000's)

A	B	C	D	E	F	G	H	I	J	K	L
8	18	2	62	51	1	5	11	38	2	1	1

In order to do the analysis, we make a new table by carrying out the following:

- **Step 1** Rewrite the table in rank order of the frequencies. We have designated the last few Other.

- **Step 2** Calculate the relative percentage for each customer (what proportion of the total 200 they represent), the cumulative frequency, and the percentage cumulative frequency. These are shown in the table below:

	Cumulative	Cumulative %	
D	62	62	31.0
E	51	113	56.5
I	38	151	75.5
B	18	169	84.5
H	11	180	90.0
A	8	188	94.0
G	5	193	96.5
J	2	195	97.5
C	2	197	98.5
Other	3	200	100.0

Even from the table it is easy to see that four customers account for 84.5 percent of the sales. This is shown more clearly if we plot the individual frequencies (against the left-hand scale), and the cumulative percentage frequency (against the right-hand scale).

If we are looking at sources of errors (as we often are with Pareto diagrams), this kind of analysis tells us where best to focus attention or remedial action. In our example, it gives us some quantitative information on which to base our decisions at the next stage. This might involve direct action—such as dropping interest in a few customers. More likely, it would involve further analysis. It would be interesting to do a similar kind of analysis on the *number* of transactions (and therefore staff time). If it turned out that some of the smaller customers used a disproportionate amount of resources, that too would be a basis for action.

DECISION MAKING

Quantitative decision making involves assessing both the probability of various occurrences or outcomes, and the value of those outcomes. An important concept in quantitative decision making is that of *expected value*.

Expected value

Suppose we want to invest $1,000. We can simplify the options and say that we can invest either in a savings and loan account or in shares. Let us say that we are in a position to estimate that, by the end of the year, the shares will have either appreciated to $1,200 or depreciated to $600.

Probabilities can be assessed in various ways. We use *subjective* probability as a best guess where there is little systematic quantitative information available. However, we can also assess probabilities by looking at the frequency of previous occurrences of the phenomenon in question. Think about the weather. For any particular day it is very difficult to know whether it will rain or not. However, by looking at past rainfall figures, we can make a good estimate of the probability of it raining on a particular day. In most business contexts also, there is a reasonable way to quantify uncertainty.

We estimate that the chances of our investment appreciating are 0.8, and that the chances of it depreciating are 0.2. In the savings and loan, it will appreciate at 10 percent. In order to compare outcomes and make a decision, we use the expected value, which here amounts to:

$$(\$1{,}200 \times 0.8) + (\$600 \times 0.2)$$
$$= \$960 + \$120$$
$$= \$1{,}080$$

The value is closer to \$1,200 than to \$600, because that former option is more likely.

The expected value of the savings and loan option is not in doubt, because there is little uncertainty or probability attached to it. It is \$1,000 plus 10 percent, which is \$1,100. Thus, on this basis we would choose the thrift and loan option. If, however, the probabilities were estimated at 0.9 and 0.1, we could recalculate the expected value as:

$$(1{,}200 \times 0.9) + (\$600 \times 0.1) = \$1{,}080 + \$60 = \$1{,}140$$

Now it would make more sense to invest in the shares. Nevertheless, the expected cash value is not always the appropriate or only measure of the desirability of an outcome. As with all investment decisions, you should only enter into it if you can afford the downside risk. In this case, although there is only a small chance of it happening, it is possible you will be faced with a substantial loss. You have to accept this risk and be able to bear the loss.

Another context in which the concept of expected value can be important is in "make or buy" decisions. These always involve an element of uncertainty, in the sense that you have to make judgments about sales or requirements.

Take the following example. A manufacturing company buys cardboard packaging for its products at a price of \$1.40. It is now investigating whether to make this packaging itself. It has enough information to be able to estimate demand as follows:

Demand	Probability
40,000	.1
60,000	.3
80,000	.4
100,000	.15
120,000	.05

To make it, the company would have to buy a cutting and folding machine, which would cost \$16,000. The materials and labor would then cost \$1 per unit. Should they make or buy?

To answer this question, you must first calculate the expected demand. This is done by multiplying the demand values by the probabilities and totaling them. This gives an expected demand of 75,000 units. Now we cost out the make and buy options for a demand of 75,000.

> To make would cost (\$16,000 + 75,000) × \$1 = \$91,000
> To buy would cost 75,000 × \$1.40 = \$105,000

Therefore it should pay to make the packaging. As always, though, such a decision should only be taken if we can afford for demand to be lower than 75,000 in the first year, and if we then expect demand to be buoyant over the coming years.

You may notice that this problem resembles the break-even analysis in Chapter 5. In fact, that is the graphical equivalent of this mathematical method, and you might like to think how you could solve it as a break-even problem.

Decision trees

The fact that you might find it useful to move between mathematical and graphic techniques in the above example gives a good introduction to the final component of our decision-making approach. ***Decision trees*** are a good method of capturing a set of complex outcomes in a systematic way, and they are particularly useful for illustrating sets of binary options, together with associated probabilities. Binary options are those options that allow *two* possible outcomes.

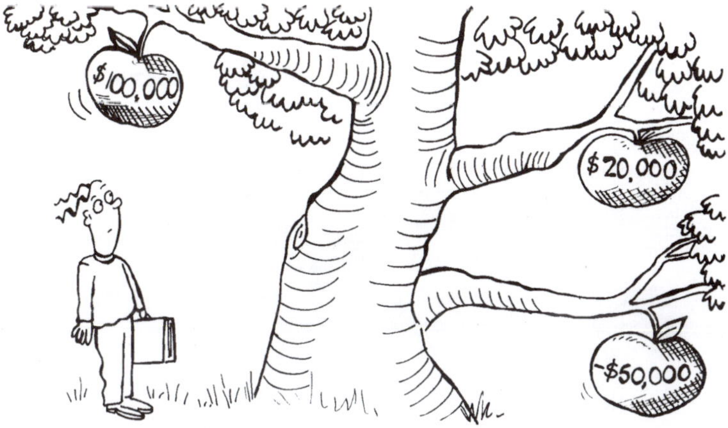

A decision tree is constructed by showing two types of option:

- decision points
- chance points

If chances are defined by probabilities and the effects can be quantified, we can calculate the expected value. For instance, we might be considering whether to rent or sell a product.

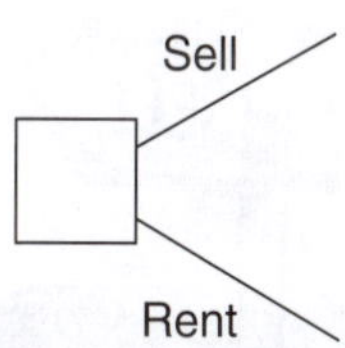

If we sell, the possible outcomes are

- very successful: we make $100,000. The probability is .5.
- successful: we make $20,000. The probability is .2.
- unsuccessful: we lose $50,000. The probability is .3.

This can be shown in a decision tree:

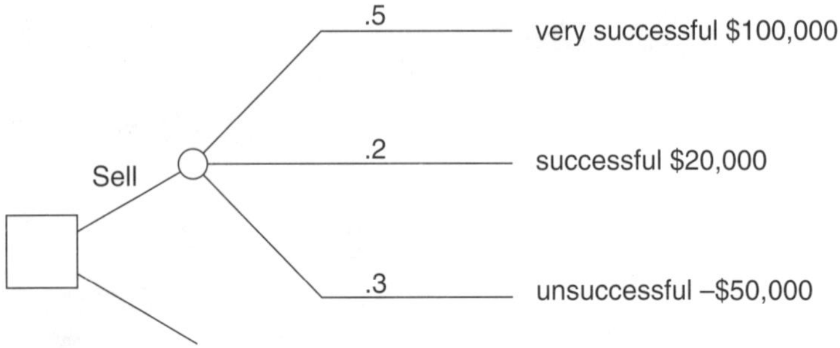

The expected values can be calculated, and totaled.

\$100,000 × .5	=	\$ 50,000
\$20,000 × .2	=	\$ 4,000
–\$50,000 × .3	=	–\$ 15,000
		\$ 39,000

By calculating all of the expected values, we are in a position to make an informed and quantified decision by comparing the outcome to the rent option.

A slightly more complex example is shown in the diagram below, which illustrates the decisions and chances involved in insuring an oil tanker.

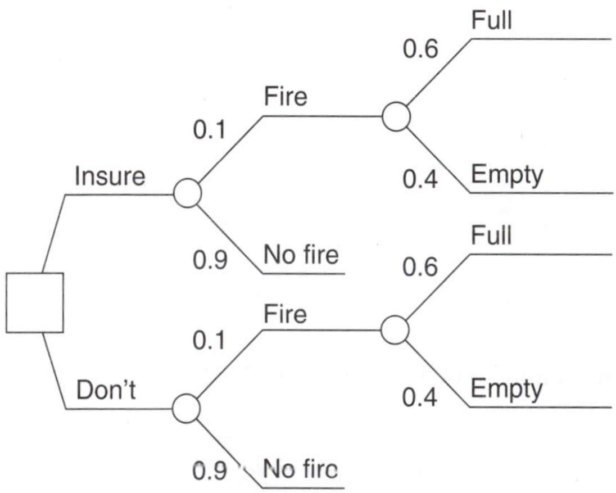

SUMMARY

We have applied some quantitative methods to problem solving and decision making in business contexts. In problem solving we used Pareto analysis to quantify priorities for causes of problems. For decision analysis we built up a model with the ideas of expected value, and showed how to illustrate options with decision trees.

We have now covered a lot of ground and set out a large number of ideas and methods. Very few people will want or need to use all of these. The purpose is to give you insight into the possibilities. If you were able to pick up just a few that you can use to help you at work, then the book (its expected value?) is a success.

TERMS AND METHODS

Mean. The mean ($\overline{x}$) of a set of data is

$$\frac{\Sigma x}{n}$$

For frequency distributions it is

$$\frac{\Sigma fx}{\Sigma f}$$

Where data is grouped we use the midpoints of the groups for the x values.

Standard deviation. The standard deviation for a set of data is

$$\sqrt{\frac{\Sigma\left(x-\overline{x}\right)^2}{n}}$$

For *grouped frequency tables* the standard deviation is

$$\sqrt{\frac{\Sigma f\left(x-\overline{x}\right)^2}{\Sigma f}}$$

This can be calculated more simply by using the formula

$$s = \sqrt{\frac{\Sigma fx^2}{\Sigma f}-\left(\frac{\Sigma fx}{\Sigma f}\right)^2}$$

Frequency distributions can take a variety of forms and shapes. The *skewness* and *kurtosis* can be described numerically. One characteristic shape that appears for many natural quantities is the normal curve.

Using graphs we can show the relationship between two variables. In *time series*, quantities are plotted against a timescale. In these cases we can identify the trend by calculating the *moving average.* A variation is the *Gannt chart,* in which we plot planned and actual performance against a time line.

Straight line graphs can also be used for other variables. In a *break-even graph* we plot costs and revenues against units. Other kinds of relationships can be identified by using *scatter diagrams.*

Most advanced statistics involves the use of *probability.* This is used to model uncertainty, and also to define confidence limits when we obtain information by *sampling.*

In problem solving, we use *Pareto analysis* to identify major factors. In decision analysis we use the notion of *expected value* to combine and evaluate probabilities and values for uncertain outcomes. These can be illustrated on a *decision tree.*

INDEX